A Literature Kit™ FOR

From the Mixed-Up Files of Mrs. Basil E. Frankweiler

By E.L. Konigsburg

Written by Michelle Jensen

GRADES 5 - 6

Classroom Complete Press
P.O. Box 19729
San Diego, CA 92159
Tel: 1-800-663-3609 | Fax: 1-800-663-3608
Email: service@classroomcompletepress.com

www.classroomcompletepress.com

ISBN – 13: 978-1-77167-247-4

© 2015

Permission to Reproduce

Pages of this publication designated as reproducible may be reproduced under licence from Access Copyright. All other pages may only be reproduced with the express written permission of Classroom Complete Press, or as permitted by law. All rights are otherwise reserved and no part of this publication may be reproduced, stored in a retrieval system, or transmitted in any form or by any means, electronic, mechanic, photocopying, scanning, recording or otherwise, except as specifically authorized. Permission is granted to the individual teacher who purchases one copy of this book to reproduce the student activity material for use in his or her classroom only. Reproduction of these materials for colleagues, an entire school or school system or for commercial sale is strictly prohibited.

We acknowledge the financial support of the Government of Canada through the Book Publishing Industry Development Program (BPIDP) for our publishing activities.

Critical Thinking Skills

From the Mixed-Up Files of Mrs. Basil E. Frankweiler

Level	Skills for Critical Thinking	Chapter Questions 1	2	3	4	5	6	7	8	9	10	Writing Tasks	Graphic Organizers
LEVEL 1 Remembering	• Identify Story Elements	✓	✓			✓	✓	✓	✓	✓	✓	✓	✓
	• Recall Details	✓	✓	✓	✓	✓	✓	✓	✓	✓	✓	✓	✓
	• Match	✓		✓									
	• Sequence Events		✓		✓			✓		✓			
LEVEL 2 Understanding	• Compare & Contrast				✓					✓			✓
	• Summarize		✓			✓		✓			✓	✓	
	• State Main Idea	✓	✓				✓			✓			
	• Describe		✓	✓	✓	✓	✓	✓	✓	✓			
	• Classify	✓							✓		✓		
LEVEL 3 Applying	• Plan			✓			✓		✓				✓
	• Interview					✓						✓	
	• Infer Outcomes	✓	✓		✓			✓	✓	✓			
LEVEL 4 Analysing	• Draw Conclusions		✓	✓	✓	✓		✓	✓	✓	✓		
	• Identify Supporting Evidence	✓	✓		✓		✓	✓		✓	✓		✓
	• Motivations	✓			✓	✓			✓		✓		
	• Identify Cause & Effect			✓		✓						✓	
LEVEL 5 Evaluating	• State & Defend An Opinion		✓			✓			✓		✓		
	• Make Judgements	✓	✓				✓	✓		✓	✓		✓
LEVEL 6 Creating	• Predict	✓	✓	✓	✓	✓		✓		✓	✓		
	• Design				✓							✓	
	• Create											✓	
	• Imagine Alternatives						✓		✓	✓		✓	

Based on Bloom's Taxonomy

Contents

✔ 6 **BONUS Activity Pages!** **Additional worksheets for your students**

FREE!

Download a digital copy for use with your projection system or interactive whiteboard

Go to our website: **www.classroomcompletepress.com/bonus**

- Enter item CC2528
- Enter pass code CC2528D for Activity Pages.

Assessment Rubric

From the Mixed-Up Files of Mrs. Basil E. Frankweiler

Student's Name: ____________ Assignment: ____________ Level: ________

	Level 1	Level 2	Level 3	Level 4
Comprehension of Novel	Demonstrates a limited understanding of the novel	Demonstrates a basic understanding of the novel	Demonstrates a good understanding of the novel	Demonstrates a thorough understanding of the novel
Content • information and details relevant to focus	Elements incomplete; key details missing	Some elements complete; details missing	All required elements completed; key details contain some description	All required elements completed; enough description for clarity
Style • effective word choice and originality • precise language	Little variety in word choice. Language vague and imprecise	Some variety in word choice. Language somewhat vague and imprecise	Good variety in word choice. Language precise and quite descriptive	Writer's voice is apparent throughout. Excellent choice of words. Precise language
Conventions • spelling, language, capitalization, punctuation	Errors seriously interfere with the writer's purpose	Repeated errors in mechanics and usage	Some errors in convention	Few errors in convention

STRENGTHS:

WEAKNESSES:

NEXT STEPS:

Teacher Guide

Our resource has been created for ease of use by both ***TEACHERS*** *and* ***STUDENTS*** *alike.*

Introduction

Our literature kit is designed to give the teacher a number of helpful ways of making the study of this novel a more enjoyable and profitable experience for the students. Our guide features a number of useful and flexible components, from which the teacher can choose. It is not expected that all of the activities will be completed.

One advantage to this approach to the study of a novel is that the student can work at his or her own speed, and the teacher can assign activities that match the student's abilities.

Our literature kit divides the novel by chapters and features reading comprehension and vocabulary questions. Themes include self-actualization, family, growing up, and growing old. From the Mixed-Up Files of Mrs. Basil E. Frankweiler *gives classrooms a chance to discuss decision-making, self-worth, self-esteem, and personal safety.*

How Is Our Literature Kit™ Organized?

STUDENT HANDOUTS

Chapter Activities *(in the form of reproducible worksheets)* make up the majority of this resource. For each group of chapters, there are BEFORE YOU READ activities and AFTER YOU READ activities.

- The BEFORE YOU READ activities prepare students for reading by setting a purpose for reading. They stimulate background knowledge and experience, and guide students to make connections between what they know and what they will learn. Important concepts and vocabulary from the chapter(s) are also presented.
- The AFTER YOU READ activities check students' comprehension and extend their learning. Students are asked to give thoughtful consideration of the text through creative and evaluative short-answer questions and journal prompts.

Six **Writing Tasks** and three **Graphic Organizers** are included to further develop students' critical thinking and writing skills, and analysis of the text. *(See page 6 for suggestions on using the Graphic Organizers.)* The **Assessment Rubric** *(page 4)* is a useful tool for evaluating students' responses to the Writing Tasks and Graphic Organizers.

PICTURE CUES

This resource contains three main types of pages, each with a different purpose and use. A **Picture Cue** at the top of each page shows, at a glance, what the page is for.

Teacher Guide
- Information and tools for the teacher

Student Handout
- Reproducible worksheets and activities

Easy Marking™ Answer Key
- Answers for student activities

EASY MARKING™ ANSWER KEY

Marking students' worksheets is fast and easy with this **Answer Key**. Answers are listed in columns—just line up the column with its corresponding worksheet, as shown, and see how every question matches up with its answer!

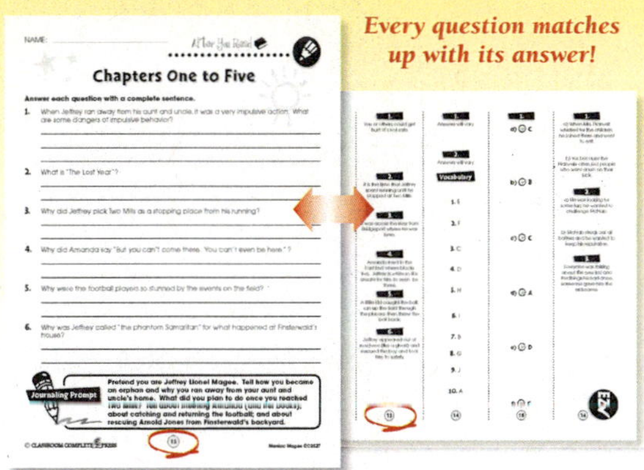

1, 2, 3

Graphic Organizers

The three **Graphic Organizers** included in this **Literature Kit™** are especially suited to a study of ***From the Mixed-Up Files of Mrs. Basil E. Frankweiler***. Below are suggestions for using each organizer in your classroom, or they may also be adapted to suit the individual needs of your students. The organizers can be used on a projection system or interactive whiteboard in teacher-led activities, small group activities, and/or photocopied for use as student worksheets. To evaluate students' responses to any of the organizers,you may wish to use the **Assessment Rubric** *(on page 4)*.

VENN DIAGRAM

There are a lot of similarities and differences between the characters in this book. For students ready for a challenge, they may choose to compare Claudia with Mrs. Basil E. Frankweiler, or Jamie and Saxonberry. Students who are just starting to learn how to gather detail from the story can compare Claudia with her brother, Jamie. Students use the Venn diagram to collect key facts while reading the story. Each circle represents one person, and where the two circles overlap, students record similarities shared by both characters. Found on Page 53.

MAP OUT THEIR JOURNEY

Students record the key elements that take place in the story. Record the introduction of the story in the family home in Greenwich. Then, describe the rising actions. At the Museum of Art in New York, write down the climax of the story. Follow this with the falling action of the story. Finish off by recording the conclusion of the story at Mrs. Frankweiler's home. Found on Page 54.

LITERARY ELEMENTS

Using the filing cabinet graphic, students gather clues while they read to help them explain literary concepts that exist outside the story. They find quotes that help to explain Literary Elements in the novel. Students use each 'file folder' to record quotes and page numbers to demonstrate the author's tone, mood, purpose, audience and writing style. Found on Page 55.

Bloom's Taxonomy* for Reading Comprehension

The activities in this resource engage and build the full range of thinking skills that are essential for students' reading comprehension. Based on the six levels of thinking in Bloom's Taxonomy, questions are given that challenge students to not only recall what they have read, but to move beyond this to understand the text through higher-order thinking. By using higher-order skills of applying, analyzing, evaluating and creating, students become active readers, drawing more meaning from the text, and applying and extending their learning in more sophisticated ways.

This **Literature Kit™**, therefore, is an effective tool for any Language Arts program. Whether it is used in whole or in part, or adapted to meet individual student needs, this resource provides teachers with the important questions to ask, inspiring students' interest and creativity, and promoting meaningful learning.

BLOOM'S TAXONOMY: 6 LEVELS OF THINKING

***Bloom's Taxonomy is a widely used tool by educators for classifying learning objectives, and is based on the work of Benjamin Bloom.**

Teaching Strategies

WHOLE-CLASS, SMALL GROUP AND INDEPENDENT STUDY

This study guide contains the following activities:

Before Reading Activities: themes are introduced and thought-provoking questions put forward for the students to consider.

Vocabulary Activities: new and unfamiliar words are introduced and reviewed.

After Reading Questions: the first part of this section includes short answer questions dealing with the content of the text. The second part features questions that are more open-ended and feature concepts from the higher order of Bloom's Taxonomy.

Writing Tasks: creative writing assignments based on Bloom's Taxonomy that relate to the plot of the particular chapters.

A comprehension quiz is also included comprised of multiple-choice, true/false and short-answer questions.

Graphic Organizers: three full-page reproducible sheets have been included and can be used for teaching purposes throughout the text.

Bonus Sheets are also available online.

The study guide can be used in a variety of ways in the classroom depending on the needs of the students and teacher. The teacher may choose to use an independent reading approach with students capable of working independently. It also works well with small groups, with most of the lessons being quite easy to follow. Finally, in other situations, teachers will choose to use it with their entire class.

Teachers may wish to have their students keep a daily reading log so that they might record their daily progress and reflections.

Summary of the Story

From the Mixed Up Files of Mrs. Basil E. Frankweiler *is told by Mrs. Basil E. Frankweiler. She writes the story to Saxonbury, her lawyer. Mrs. Basil E. Frankweiler tells about the main character, Claudia. Claudia is a strong, intelligent young girl. The problem is that Claudia feels ordinary. Claudia wants to feel important. She wants to be more than just an older sister in a New York suburb. She decides to do something extraordinary. Claudia doesn't run away, she decides to run to some place. She selects the most interesting place she can find. She talks younger brother into running to the Metropolitan Museum of Art with her. She could live in comfort there until she was ready to return home. After careful planning, Claudia and her brother Jamie leave home and live in the Museum. At the museum, they see a beautiful stone-sculptured Angel. There is a mystery about who made the statue. The two children decide to solve the mystery. Claudia believes that solving the mystery will make her 'important'. During the investigation, Claudia and Jamie meet Mrs. Basil E. Frankweiler. Mrs. Frankweiler is also the last owner of the stone statue. At the end of the story, Claudia and Jamie learn who sculpted the stone angel. The reader also learns why Mrs. Basil E. Frankweiler was the person telling the story. In the end, Claudia can go home feeling special. She learns a valuable life lesson.*

Suggestions for Further Reading

OTHER BOOKS BY E.L. KONIGSBURG

Jennifer, Hecate, Macbeth, William McKinley and Me, Elizabeth *© 1967*

About the B'nai Bagels *© 1969*

A Proud Taste for Scarlet and Miniver *© 1973*

The Dragon in the Ghetto Caper *© 1974*

Father's Arcane Daughter *© 1976*

Journey to an 800 Number *© 1982*

Up From Jericho Tel *© 1986*

OTHER RECOMMENDED RESOURCES

Mary Norton, ***The Borrowers*** © 1953

Norton Juster, ***The Phantom Tollbooth*** © 1961

Madeleine L'Engle, ***A Wrinkle in Time*** © 1962

Betsy Byars, ***The Summer of the Swans*** © 1970

Katherine Paterson, ***The Great Gilly Hopkins*** © 1978

Ann Rinaldi, ***A Stitch in Time*** © 1985

Rebecca Stead, ***When You Reach Me*** © 2009

List of Vocabulary

CHAPTER 1
• monotony • injustice • suburbs • knapsack • commuting • Mah-Jong • ventured • exhausting • jostling • Neanderthal • fiscal week • vow • tyrannies • tycoon • cautious

CHAPTER 2
• thoroughness • percolator • sissy • expenditures • terminal • ragged • racket

CHAPTER 3
• extravagant • cheapskate • accumulation • carbon dioxide • mimicked • inconspicuous • veto • tyrannical • tightwad • Chancellor of the Exchequer • spendthrift

CHAPTER 4
• peculiar • dreaded • petticoat • whiffs • essence • stash • sarcophagus • tapestry • urn • drape• manning • corridors • emerge • automat • enormous • outrageous • galleries • despair • glorification • barrier • a vain effort • inconspicuous • encountered • imposter • vat • smug • glimpse • acquisition • hodgepodge • mediocre • smoldering

CHAPTER 5
• persuade • discourage • directory • executive ability • juvenile delinquent • genius • pagan • worshipping idols • humbled • humility • irritable • dope • lag time • emerge • corpuscle • peck of potatoes • mental telepathy • dost • well adjusted

CHAPTER 6
• furious • pinchpenny • Congressional Medal of Honor • shepherded • descending • telegram • stealthily • quarters • stonemason

CHAPTER 7
• quarterly • urged • treasurer • scowled • anxious • mastaba • vacuum of time • stowaways • pharaoh • drizzle • muzzled • mysterious • sock

CHAPTER 8
• derby • flavored • topaz • keen • heroine • counterfeited • altar • consensus • appreciate • disclosing • sarcastic • righteously • fidgeted • hunch

CHAPTER 9
• paupers • ascended • intrigued • chandeliers • formica • florescence • baroque • emitted • theatrics • kaleidoscope • manila folder • cherish • frantic • suicide • commotion • astounded • charity • blabbermouth • chauffeur • handicap • exhausted • sauntered • sonnet • emerged • boodle • jittering • authenticity • deceased • caper

CHAPTER 10
• preoccupied • maimed • accurate • intercom • tight • auction • matron • bequeathing • chariot

E.L. Konigsburg

E.L. Konigsburg was born Elaine Lobl on February 10, 1930. She grew up most of her life in small towns in Pennsylvania. She was the first person in her family to attend college, where she studied Chemistry. She became Elaine Lobl Konigsburg when she married her husband David Konigsburg, who she had met while at college. She taught chemistry for a short time at a school in Florida; but when she had children, she stayed home to raise them, and that's when her inner artist began to bloom.

E.L. Konigsburg began to take art lessons when her children were very young. She took these lessons on Saturday mornings, and spent many Saturday afternoons exploring the Metropolitan Museum of Art. This museum would serve as the setting for much of her novel, *From the Mixed-Up Files of Mrs. Basil E. Frankweiler.*

When her children started school, Konigsburg started writing. Her desire to write came from a combination of her life experiences. As a child, she hadn't been able to identify with any of the characters in the books she read. As a parent, she wanted to have characters in books for them to enjoy and with whom they could connect. As a teacher, she had been very interested in what was happening for the students in her classes. She noticed that young people wanted to be both accepted as part of the group, but also to stand out as individuals. This would serve as a common message in her novel, *From the Mixed-Up Files of Mrs. Basil E. Frankweiler.* She also wanted to create examples of writing that would enrich young people's lives; often through introduction to amazing artists, colorful characters and the spirit of adventure, or to common human virtues, including kindness, curiosity and encouragement.

Did You Know?

- **In 1968, she won the Newbery Medal for *From the Mixed-Up Files of Mrs. Basil E. Frankweiler* and the Newbery Honor award for *Jennifer, Hecate, Macbeth, William McKinley and Me, Elizabeth.***
- **Is the first author to win both the Newbery Medal and Newbery Honor award in the same year.**
- **Her advice to children is: "Before you can be anything, you have to be yourself. That's the hardest thing to find.**

© CLASSROOM COMPLETE PRESS

NAME: ______________________

Chapter One

Answer the questions in complete sentences.

1. Who do you think "Mrs. Basil E. Frankweiler" will be?

____

____

2. Have you ever wanted to run away from home? What were your reasons?

____

____

Vocabulary

With a straight line, connect each word on the left with its meaning on the right.

1	**monotony**	to travel from home to work and back again	A
2	**Mah Jong**	to bump up against people in a crowd	B
3	**commuting**	not fair	C
4	**injustice**	when something is the same all the time	D
5	**fiscal week**	a very rich person	E
6	**suburbs**	a promise to yourself	F
7	**jostling**	towns just outside of a big city	G
8	**ventured**	tried	H
9	**tycoon**	the start of 7 days of keeping track of money being spent	I
10	**vow**	a type of game from China	J

After You Read

NAME: ______________________________

Chapter One

1. Put a check mark (✓) next to the answer that is most correct.

a) For how long did Claudia save her allowance, so she could have money to run away?

- ◯ **A** 1 week
- ◯ **B** 2 weeks
- ◯ **C** 3 weeks
- ◯ **D** 4 weeks

b) What did Claudia find in the waste basket that allowed them to run away the next week?

- ◯ **A** money
- ◯ **B** a map of the city
- ◯ **C** a museum brochure
- ◯ **D** a train ticket

c) How many brothers does Claudia have?

- ◯ **A** 1
- ◯ **B** 2
- ◯ **C** 3
- ◯ **D** 4

d) What did Claudia say she wanted Jamie to do?

- ◯ **A** share an adventure
- ◯ **B** stop playing cards
- ◯ **C** look after Kevin
- ◯ **D** skip school

e) Why does Jamie have more money than Claudia thought possible?

- ◯ **A** He gambles with Bruce.
- ◯ **B** He delivers papers.
- ◯ **C** He steals Kevin's allowance.
- ◯ **D** He saves his money.

NAME: ______________________________

After You Read

Chapter One

Answer each question with a complete sentence.

1. In who's point of view is the story being told? Explain your reasoning.

____

____

2. Describe Claudia's personality. Find quotes from the story to support your description.

____

____

3. Why does Claudia want to run away? Give at least 2 reasons using quotes from the story to prove your opinion.

____

____

____

4. Compare Claudia with her brother Jamie. How are they the same? How are they different?

____

____

5. What are 3 reasons why Claudia chose Jamie as her runaway partner?

____

____

6. When authors hint at what is going to happen, it is called foreshadowing. Find a quote at the end of the Chapter that foreshadows the next event in the book.

____

____

If you could plan an adventure, where would you go? What would you need for the trip? How would you get there? Why would you want to go there? With whom would you want to go? Create a plan that answers each of these questions.

NAME: ______________________

Chapter Two

Answer the questions in complete sentences.

1. In the last Chapter, we find out that Claudia can't really remember why she wanted to run away. Why do you think she still wants to run away?

____

2. Do you think an Art museum would be a good place to 'run to'? Explain.

____

____

Vocabulary **Complete each sentence with a word from the list.**

thoroughness	Traveler's Checks	expenditures	ragged
percolator	sissy	terminal	racket

1. A way to describe a rough ride is to call it a ____________ ride.
2. One way to make coffee is to put the ground up coffee in the top of the coffee maker, and put water in the bottom of the carafe. Then heat the water to a boil, so it will be pushed up through a small tube into the top of the coffee maker, and down into the coffee grounds. This is called a ____________.
3. When something makes a lot of noise, you could say it makes a ____________
4. If you have something to do, and you look at all the details, to finish the work completely, then you could say that you showed ____________ in your work.
5. ____________ is a fancy way of saying the way you spend your money.
6. The end of the line for trains is the ____________.
7. ____________ is a slang word for someone being a bit immature or easily frightened or weak-willed.
8. A safe way to carry money on a trip is to buy ____________. They are safe because if they are lost or stolen, they can be replaced.

Chapter Two

1. Number the events from 1 to 7 in the order they occurred in the Chapter.

- ☐ **a)** The children hid on the school bus on Wednesday morning, when all the other children got off the bus to go to school.
- ☐ **b)** Claudia mailed 2 letters before getting on the train.
- ☐ **c)** Jamie tried to convince Claudia to hide in Central Park instead of the Metropolitan Museum of Art.
- ☐ **d)** The two Kincaid children took the train to New York City.
- ☐ **e)** Claudia and Jamie packed their clothes in their music cases on Tuesday night.
- ☐ **f)** Jamie tried to eat the paper of instructions that Claudia had written.
- ☐ **g)** On Tuesday night, Jamie found a list of instructions pinned to his pajamas.

2. Circle T if the statement is TRUE or F if it is FALSE.

- T F **a)** Claudia told Jamie to finish his homework.
- T F **b)** Jamie burned the note that Claudia gave him.
- T F **c)** Jamie thought they were running away to live in the woods.
- T F **d)** Claudia wanted to take a taxi to New York City.
- T F **e)** Jamie wanted to hitchhike to New York City.
- T F **f)** Jamie brought $30.24.
- T F **g)** Claudia appointed Jamie treasurer, so he would keep track of the money.
- T F **h)** When they arrived in New York City, Claudia wished that she had come alone.

After You Read

NAME: ______________________

Chapter Two

Answer each question with a complete sentence.

1. What does the narrator mean when she writes, "I wholeheartedly admire Claudia's thoroughness"?

2. Why did Jamie insist on trying to eat the instructions? What does that tell you about him?

3. What is the importance of Claudia mailing the cereal box tops away? What does that tell us of her plans?

4. Why did Jamie bring his compass? What does that tell you about his idea of 'the greatest adventure of his life'?

5. What does it mean when the narrator writes, "Ah how well I know those feelings of hot and hollow that come from the dimly lit concrete ramp"?

6. In the end of this Chapter, as the children arrive at Grand Central Station, why is Claudia happy to have Jamie with her on this trip?

Think of a time when you went somewhere and you needed courage. Write about a time when you were glad to have a friend or family member with you on a trip. Describe the trip, and why it helped to have company. Imagine what your trip would have been like alone. How might that have changed your feelings about the trip?

NAME: ______________________

Chapter Three

Answer the questions in complete sentences.

1. Even though the two children are quite different, why might they be a good 'adventure' team?

____

____

____

2. What problems can you predict for Claudia and Jamie, now that they have arrived in the big city?

____

____

Vocabulary

Choose a word from the list that means the same or nearly the same as the underlined words.

extravagant	accumulation	mimicked	veto
cheapskate	carbon dioxide	inconspicuous	tyrannical

[ ] 1. He **imitated** her.

[ ] 2. She spent a lot of money. She was a **spendthrift**.

[ ] 3. He had his **collection** of toys on display.

[ ] 4. He was very stingy, some even called him a **miser**.

[ ] 5. Cars that burn gas and give off **gas**.

[ ] 6. He has the **power to say no** to all decisions.

[ ] 7. She was **blending in with the crowd**.

[ ] 8. He was **like a dictator**.

NAME: ____________________

Chapter Three

1. Put a check mark (✓) next to the answer that is most correct.

a) Why is Claudia annoyed with Jamie?

- ◯ **A** He made her walk.
- ◯ **B** She has muscle fatigue.
- ◯ **C** He has a compass.
- ◯ **D** Her violin case is hitting his trumpet case.

b) Why does Jamie say Claudia is brilliant?

- ◯ **A** He loves the shops on Fifth Avenue.
- ◯ **B** No on notices you in New York.
- ◯ **C** She walked all the way to the museum.
- ◯ **D** She was dressed inconspicuously.

c) What time did Claudia and Jamie arrive at the museum?

- ◯ **A** 10:14
- ◯ **B** 11:07
- ◯ **C** 12:30
- ◯ **D** 1:00

d) Why did Jamie have to wear his ski jacket around?

- ◯ **A** It hid the sound of his coins.
- ◯ **B** He was still cold from the long walk.
- ◯ **C** He didn't want to lose it.
- ◯ **D** He was trying to be inconspicuous.

e) What are Jamie and Claudia worried about?

- ◯ **A** Their clothes and instrument cases.
- ◯ **B** Money.
- ◯ **C** Food.
- ◯ **D** Their parents might be worried about them.

f) Where did Claudia and Jamie wait until the museum closed?

- ◯ **A** Hall of the English Renaissance.
- ◯ **B** Bathrooms by the restaurant.
- ◯ **C** The Children's Museum.
- ◯ **D** The lunch counter downstairs.

NAME: ______________________

Chapter Three

Answer each question with a complete sentence.

1. List all the types of people who come to visit the museum on a typical Wednesday.

2. Why do you think the narrator—Mrs. Basil E. Frankweiler—goes to such length to describe the different types of visitors who visit the museum in pairs?

3. Why is the narrator badgering Saxonberg? Who is Saxonberg?

4. How did Claudia arrange for them to be in the museum at night with their belongings? How will they avoid the night watchmen and the security system?

5. Why were the children so tired that they fell asleep shortly after 6 p.m.?

6. Why didn't the night watchman catch Claudia and Jamie?

In some cities, there are 'sleepovers' available in public sites: the Zoo, the Aquatic Center, Recreation Center, Science Museums, Planetarium/Observatory, the Aquarium, etc. What would you do if you could spend a night in a public building? Where would you spend your night? What would you bring? What would you do? Who would you invite with you? Outline your perfect 'sleepover'.

NAME: ______________________

Chapter Four

Vocabulary

automat	emerge	glorification	petticoat	stash
barrier	enormous	hodge	sarcophagus	urn
drape	essence	imposter	smoldering	vat
dreaded	glimpse	mediocre	smug	whiff

Across	Down
1. Huge or immense.	2. So-so, not really horrible or great.
3. When you would like to avoid something.	4. Another word for curtain.
6. A large stone coffin.	5. The real true nature of something that determines its character.
10. To move out of something and come into view.	7. A quick look at something.
12. _______ Podge: an unusual assortment of items.	8. To burn slowly.
13. A quick sniff.	9. An old-fashioned slip that went under a dress or skirt.
14. A large vase.	11. To hold something up to be appreciated.
15. To hide something quickly.	15. To be proud.
18. Someone who is not who they say they are.	16. A restaurant made up of vending machines.
19. A huge container for making or storing.	17. A fence or rope that prevents entrance to an area.

NAME: ______________________________

Chapter Four

1. Fill in each blank with the correct word(s) from the Chapter.

a) They agreed to __________ their belongings. Thus, if the museum __________ found one thing, they wouldn't necessarily find all.

b) Claudia hid her violin case in a __________ that had no lid. She hid her book bag behind a __________ screen in the rooms of French furniture. The trumpet case was hidden inside a huge __________ and Jamie's book bag was neatly tucked behind a __________ that was behind a statue from the Middle Ages.

c) Jamie made one __________ error that morning.... It was not, however, a museum __________ who had turned on the water tap. It was a __________ filling his bucket. He was leaning down in the act of __________ out his mop when he saw Jamie's legs appear from nowhere and then saw Jamie emerge.

d) Jamie smiled and nodded. "Mother always says that I came from Heaven." He bowed politely and walked out ________ with his brush with ________.

e) Claudia especially wanted to make herself __________ to the statue. She would solve its __________ and it, in turn, would do something important to her, though what this was, she didn't quite know.

2. Number the events from 1 to 6 in the order they occurred in the Chapter.

☐ **a)** Claudia and Jamie walk past the statue of the angel.

☐ **b)** The children find out there is a mystery about the angel.

☐ **c)** Jamie tries to get his picture taken by a newspaper reporter.

☐ **d)** Jamie got mad because Claudia pushed him.

☐ **e)** The children want to find out everything they can about who carved the statue.

☐ **f)** Jamie and Claudia steal a New York Times newspaper.

NAME: ___________________________

Chapter Four

Answer each question with a complete sentence.

1. Find the simile used to describe how hungry the children are in the morning.

2. Claudia and Jamie find 3 new problems in this Chapter. What were they, and how did they solve them?

3. Why did Jamie choose the galleries of the Italian Renaissance to study?

4. What do you find out about Saxonberg in this Chapter based on the comments Mrs. Basil E. Frankweiler addresses to him in her writing?

5. Claudia said that she didn't like being responsible for her younger siblings. How does her behavior in this Chapter contradict that?

6. "I truly believe that his name has magic even now; the best kind of magic because it comes from true greatness. Claudia sensed it as she again stood in line. The mystery only intrigued her, the magic trapped her." Explain what the narrator means by this comment.

The Metropolitan Museum of Art has many different styles of art. There are arts and crafts from America. There is art from Ancient Egypt, Greece and Rome. Art from Italy in the 1600's called Italian renaissance. There is an Islamic Art section. There are even weapons in the Arms and Armory section. Describe what you would want to study and/or learn about if you were with Claudia. Why?

NAME: ______________________

Chapter Five

Answer the questions in complete sentences.

1. Why do you think the children haven't thought about their parents or their family?

____

____

____

2. How would this story be different if it were taking place in today's time?

____

____

____

Vocabulary

With a straight line, connect each word on the left with its meaning on the right.

1	**persuade**	do	A
2	**directory**	psychic messages	B
3	**genius**	sway	C
4	**dope**	wait time	D
5	**lag time**	list	E
6	**corpuscle**	smart	F
7	**mental telepathy**	cell	G
8	**dost**	drugs	H

NAME: ______________________________

Chapter Five

1. Put a check mark (✓) next to the answer that is most correct.

a) How long have Claudia and Jamie been away from home?

- ◯ **A** 3 days
- ◯ **B** a week
- ◯ **C** 10 days
- ◯ **D** a month

b) What did Claudia say Saturday was a good day for?

- ◯ **A** Playing in the park.
- ◯ **B** A bath.
- ◯ **C** Eating at a restaurant.
- ◯ **D** Chores.

c) Why was their laundry gray?

- ◯ **A** They didn't have soap.
- ◯ **B** The drier worked for 10 minutes.
- ◯ **C** They washed all the clothes together.
- ◯ **D** They only had gray clothes.

d) What did they do in the morning?

- ◯ **A** Played in the park.
- ◯ **B** Did laundry.
- ◯ **C** Ate.
- ◯ **D** Studied.

e) Why didn't Claudia want Jamie to eat the chocolate bar?

- ◯ **A** It could be filled with drugs.
- ◯ **B** It wasn't healthy.
- ◯ **C** It would spoil his dinner.
- ◯ **D** She wanted it all.

f) Where did Claudia and Jamie hide every morning?

- ◯ **A** In the bathroom.
- ◯ **B** In the sarcophagus.
- ◯ **C** Under a bed.
- ◯ **D** Behind a curtain.

© CLASSROOM COMPLETE PRESS

NAME: ______________________________

Chapter Five

Answer each question with a complete sentence.

1. Now that Claudia is getting to know her brother, what would Claudia say is the most important skill that Jamie has added to their adventure? Use evidence from the story to support your opinion.

2. Why do you think the author put in the scene with the chocolate bar? Give two reasons.

3. Why does Claudia want to 'hug' the statue? What does she say is the reason? What does this tell you about Claudia?

4. How do Claudia and Jamie explain their lack of homesickness?

5. Why does Claudia say: "I'm glad you asked that about homesickness, Jamie. Somehow, I feel older now."? Why is it important for her to feel older?

Do you get homesick? Write a paragraph describing when you were homesick. What did you do about it? If not, explain why you didn't feel homesick.

NAME: ______________________

Chapter Six

Answer the questions in complete sentences.

1. What is the relationship between Mrs. Basil E. Frankweiler and the Angel?

____

____

____

2. Now that the children have found a source of money at the museum, how might their behaviors change?

____

____

____

Vocabulary

Complete each sentence with a word from the list.

furious	**telegram**	**stealthily**	**stonemason**
descending	**pinchpenny**	**quarters**	**shepherded**

1. They tiptoed ______________ up the stairs after the guard had left.
2. Hiding under the bed was close ____________, Jamie could hardly move.
3. The ______________ would carve his mark on the bottom of the marble, to prove it was his.
4. The teacher __________________ her class through the museum, being sure no one was left behind.
5. In the old days, messages were sent as _________________, before telephones were popular.
6. Taking two stairs at a time, they were ___________________ down to the basement.
7. She was so ____________________. How dare he make fun of her!
8. What a ______________! He wouldn't even give her 10 cents for a newspaper.

NAME: ______________________________

Chapter Six

1. Circle **T** if the statement is TRUE or **F** if it is FALSE.

- T F **a)** Claudia insisted that they go to Church on Sunday morning.
- T F **b)** Claudia was furious with Jamie because he made fun of her.
- T F **c)** Jamie noticed that the plush from the velvet rings was crushed down.
- T F **d)** Claudia writes a letter to the head of the museum.
- T F **e)** Jamie wants to go home.
- T F **f)** Claudia wants to be different before she goes home.
- T F **g)** The children type their note at the library.
- T F **h)** Claudia signed the note: Friends of the Museum.

2. **Fill in each blank with the correct word(s) from the Chapter.**

a) The children almost get caught twice: once while looking at the ______________. Later the guard was delayed outside by the crowds, so they were not caught hiding under the velvet-covered table.

b) The children notice 3 ______________ and the letter M imprinted on the velvet table cloth.

c) They find out that this mark was used by Michelangelo's ______________.

d) They decide to write a ______________ to the museum.

After You Read

NAME: ___________________________

Chapter Six

Answer each question with a complete sentence.

1. How does Jamie tease his sister? What does this tell you about Jamie's understanding of his sister?

2. Claudia thought that Jamie was logical. Give 2 examples from the story that shows Jamie's logical thinking.

3. "Claudia didn't think about their close calls. They were unimportant; they wouldn't matter in the end, the end having something to do with Michelangelo, Angel, history, and herself." How does this quote relate to the theme of self-actualization (developing your full potential)?

4. For Claudia, the end of the adventure doesn't come with solving the mystery. What does she need to allow her to go home? Find a quote from the story to support your opinion.

5. Claudia and Jamie are developing a closer relationship. At the beginning of the story, they didn't seem to know each other very well. Find two examples from the Chapter that demonstrates the kind of relationship they have now.

Claudia says she wants to be different before she goes home. Claudia wants to be a hero. She talks about people who win the Congressional Medal of Honor or an Academy Award. What would you like to do with your life to be important? Write a paragraph explaining what you would do if you could.

NAME: ______________________

Chapter Seven

Answer the questions with a complete sentence.

1. How were Claudia and Jamie going to stay 'anonymous' and why?

____

____

____

Vocabulary

With a straight line, connect each word on the left with its meaning on the right.

1	**quarterly**	to force someone to stay quiet	A
2	**urged**	to be nervous	B
3	**scowled**	to encourage someone to do something	C
4	**anxious**	the title of a king from ancient Egypt	D
5	**mastaba**	a light rain, or smattering of something	E
6	**stowaways**	to frown in anger or annoyance	F
7	**muzzled**	slang for to punch someone	G
8	**sock**	one fourth of a year	H
9	**drizzled**	an ancient Egyptian tomb	I
10	**pharaoh**	hiding away for free rides or a place to stay	J

After You Read

NAME: ______________________

Chapter Seven

1. Number the events from 1 to 7 in the order they occurred in the Chapter.

☐ **a)** They heard the voices of students from their school.

☐ **b)** Jamie delivered the letter himself.

☐ **c)** They waited in the Egyptian tomb.

☐ **d)** Claudia said: "We'll take a long bath tonight."

☐ **e)** They took a bus to the post office.

☐ **f)** They tried to find a young student to take the letter to the museum office.

☐ **g)** Jamie paid $4.50 for a rental of a post office box.

2. Fill in each blank with the correct words from the Chapter.

a) Claudia was very impatient to rent a ____________, so they skipped ____________ and went straight to the post office.

b) At the museum, Claudia and Jamie wanted to find a ___________ who could take the letter to the museum office. They waited in the ______________ for a school group to pass.

c) Mrs. Basil E. Frankweiler ___________ to spend time in the Egyptian tomb. While in there, she said you would experience a different ____________.

d) The Kincaids were waiting in the ____________ when they heard the voice of Jaime's 3rd grade ________________.

e) Jamie was furious when Claudia _________ her hand on his mouth. She should know he would not have ______________.

f) Claudia thinks it's________________ that Jamie's class is at the museum. Now he can just deliver the ______________ himself.

g) Claudia grabs Jamie when he comes out of the office. He was so nervous, he ______________ and yelled ______________.

NAME: ______________________

Chapter Seven

Answer each question with a complete sentence.

1. What was Claudia's motive for delivering a letter to the museum? Why was Claudia so keen to get the letter delivered right away to the museum office?

2. How is Claudia's new plan to get the letter to the officials at the museum so perfect?

3. Why was Jamie so nervous after taking the letter into the museum office?

4. They have gone to great lengths to get their note to people at the museum, and have a place for the museum to respond to them. Why didn't they just go into the office and tell them what they knew? Give 3 reasons.

5. There are many coincidences and lucky breaks that help the children run away to the Museum and live there. How might coincidences support a central theme about fate?

Have you ever done something that made you feel worried about getting caught? Write a descriptive paragraph to show how you felt. Think about all your senses: what did you hear, feel, think, taste, see?

NAME: ___________________________

Chapter Eight

Answer the questions in complete sentences.

1. Claudia and Jamie are very keen to have an answer to their letter. Have you ever been impatient waiting for an answer? Describe the situation and why you were impatiently waiting. What can you do to help pass the time while you wait?

____

____

2. How do you think Mrs. Basil E. Frankweiler got a copy of the letter that Claudia typed?

____

____

Vocabulary

Complete each sentence with a word from the list.

topaz	**counterfeited**	**appreciate**	**sarcastic**	**fidgeted**
keen	**consensus**	**disclosing**	**righteously**	

1. They made ______________ money: it looked real, but was fake.

2. The ________ is a semi-precious gemstone that ranges in color from yellow to light brown.

3. He had a ________ sense of hearing: he could hear a pin drop.

4. She was very ______________ when she said: "Oh I love your sweater!", when she really meant the opposite.

5. They came to a ___________ by all agreeing to go to the movies.

6. Thank you so much! I ___________ everything you have done for me.

7. He was __________ angry that they had treated him so unfairly.

8. While waiting in the principal's office, she _____________, wondering why she was called into the office.

9. It was difficult telling people what had happened without ___________ where they had stayed.

NAME: ______________________________

Chapter Eight

1. Circle T if the statement is TRUE or F if it is FALSE.

T F **a)** On Monday the Kincaids rented a mailbox and on Tuesday they had a letter in it.

T F **b)** They did their laundry on Tuesday morning, to help pass the time.

T F **c)** They went to the United Nations Building to hide from their class.

T F **d)** Jamie said they could go on the U.N. tour if Claudia gives up her dessert.

T F **e)** Jamie tells the ticket clerk there is no school because the school burned down.

T F **f)** Claudia learned a lot about the United Nations.

T F **g)** The Museum wrote to say that they already knew about the marks on the base of the statue.

T F **h)** Jamie wants to go home because their clothes are all gray.

T F **i)** Claudia doesn't remember how to get home.

T F **j)** They decide to buy tickets to visit Mrs. Basil E. Frankweiler.

2. List facts that hint Angel was sculpted by Michelangelo and facts that hint Angel was sculpted by someone else.

Michelangelo DID sculpt Angel	Michelangelo DID NOT sculpt Angel

After You Read

NAME: ____________________

Chapter Eight

Answer each question with a complete sentence.

1. The longer they stay at the Museum of Art, the more chances they have in getting caught. Who might start to notice them? What might make them more conspicuous?

____

____

2. At the United Nations, what 2 ways did Claudia discover herself to be 'different'?

____

____

3. "Claudia would have felt better if the letter had not been so polite." Explain the meaning of this quote.

____

____

4. What was Jamie's motivation for coming on the trip? How does this make it possible for him to return home now?

____

____

5. What was Claudia's reason for coming on the adventure? How does this make it difficult to return home?

____

____

6. In what way did each of the characters change?

____

____

Dangerous behaviors: The children in this story do many things that are dangerous. Imagine you are their parents. What would you tell them about running away? What would you tell them about eating food that they found on the street? What would you tell them about wandering the streets of a big city?

NAME: ______________________

Chapter Nine

Answer the questions in complete sentences.

1. What do you know about Mrs. Frankweiler from the story so far? Give at least 4 details.

____

____

2. What do you expect Mrs. Frankweiler will be like when she meets the children for the first time?

____

____

Vocabulary

With a straight line, connect each word on the left with its meaning on the right.

1	**paupers**	went up	A
2	**ascended**	someone who can't keep a secret	B
3	**chauffeur**	to be at a disadvantage	C
4	**handicap**	people who are poor	D
5	**sauntered**	a driver	E
6	**emerged**	to stroll in casually	F
7	**jittering**	to come out of	G
8	**authenticity**	jumpy, quick movements or sounds	H
9	**cherish**	real or genuine, not copied or faked	I
10	**blabbermouth**	to hold something or someone dear	J

© CLASSROOM COMPLETE PRESS

NAME: ______________________________

Chapter Nine

1. Put a check mark (✓) next to the answer that is most correct.

a) Why does Jamie give all his money to the taxi driver?

- ○ **A** Claudia told him to.
- ○ **B** They didn't have enough for anything else anyway.
- ○ **C** He wanted to tip him.
- ○ **D** The taxi was expensive.

b) What did Jamie say to get them in to meet with Mrs. Basil E. Frankweiler?

- ○ **A** They wanted to talk about the Italian Renaissance.
- ○ **B** They wanted to know who sculpted the Angel.
- ○ **C** They wanted her help to get home.
- ○ **D** They wanted to see her evidence that Michelangelo carved the stone Angel.

c) Why does Claudia take a bath before lunch?

- ○ **A** She wants an 'elegant' experience.
- ○ **B** She was really dirty.
- ○ **C** She wanted to make them hold lunch.
- ○ **D** She had never seen a bathtub like that one.

d) Claudia would not give any details about their trip until Mrs. Basil E. Frankweiler...

- ○ **A** serves macaroni and cheese.
- ○ **B** offers to give them a ride home.
- ○ **C** plays cards with Jamie.
- ○ **D** tells them the secret about Angel.

e) Why does Claudia's habit of correcting Jamie's grammar actually help them solve the mystery?

- ○ **A** Jamie says Bologna.
- ○ **B** Claudia calls Jamie Blabbermouth.
- ○ **C** Mrs Frankweiler said "nouilles".
- ○ **D** Claudia said STOP.

NAME: ______________________________

Chapter Nine

Answer each question with a complete sentence.

1. Compare Mrs. Frankweiler's house to her office. Use details from the story. Why do you think her office is so different from the rest of her house?

____

____

2. Why do you think Mrs. Frankweiler made the children wait before she turned around to talk with them?

____

____

3. Describe Mrs. Frankweiler. What does she look like? What is her personality like? How does she speak to the children? What does she value? What does she like and dislike?

____

____

4. Why does Mrs. Frankweiler say, "Good for you!" when Claudia refuses to tell her where they have been all week?

____

____

5. What was the test that Mrs. Frankweiler set up for the children to find the answer to the mystery of the stone angel?

____

____

6. How would the story change if Mrs. Frankweiler told Claudia right away about the origin of Angel?

____

____

What makes you special or different? Think about your talents, skills, past experiences, beliefs, and personality. How are you different from everyone else?

NAME: ______________________

Chapter Ten

Answer the questions in complete sentences.

1. How do you think the author will finish up the story?

____

____

2. Claudia feels that she can go home now that she is different? How is Claudia different? How is she the same?

____

____

Vocabulary **Complete each sentence with a word from the list.**

preoccupied	accurate	tight	matron	chariot
maimed	intercom	auction	bequeathing	

1. She pressed a button and spoke into the ____________ and suddenly the butler arrived with lunch!

2. He was very careful to add up all the costs so he could have an ____________ budget.

3. She was very ____________; her mind was on something else.

4. "My grandpa came back from the war ____________. He learned to use a prosthetic leg."

5. "In my last will and testament, I am ____________ all my money."

6. The ____________ was about 55 years old, a nurse and she took control of the situation immediately.

7. On the walls in the Egyptian temple of Karnak, there is a carving of Pharaoh riding in a ____________ going out to war.

8. He was very ____________ with his money: people called him a miser.

9. "Do you like my sculpture? I bought it at an ____________."

NAME: ______________________________

Chapter Ten

1. Fill in each blank with the correct word(s) from the Chapter.

a) Claudia recorded her side of the adventure into a ______________.

b) Saxonberg contacted the ______________ of Claudia and Jamie.

c) Claudia and Mrs. Frankweiler enjoyed the ______________ of her house.

d) Sheldon was the ______________ of the limousine who drove them home.

e) During the ride, Claudia wondered why did Mrs. Frankweiler sell ______________.

f) Claudia finally decided that she sold the Angel for ______________. "Because after a time having a ______________ and nobody knowing you have a secret is no ______________."

g) The children decide to save their money so they can go back and visit ______________.

h) "We'll ____ ________ her," the girl suggested... "She'll become our grandmother with never becoming a mother first."

2. Matching: Who said this... write the character's name in the blank for each statement or quote.

________	**1.** "The game cost me thirty-four cents. I still don't know how he does it."
________	**2.** "He seemed to regard the button panel, madam, as some sort of typewriter or piano or I.B.M. computer."
________	**3.** "Maybe she didn't have room for it anymore."
________	**4.** "There's something about our running away that I forgot to say into the tape recorder."
________	**5.** "Do you think she meant that stuff about motherhood?"
________	**6.** "And that will be our secret that we won't even share with her. She'll be the only woman in the world to become a grandmother with never becoming a mother first."
________	**7.** "Boy! What a car. Hey Claude, I'll be your 'sponsibility the rest of....."
________	**8.** "Most of it was going towards increased security for the Metropolitan Museum".

NAME: ______________________

Chapter Ten

Answer each question with a complete sentence.

1. Do you think that the children will go see Mrs. Frankweiler in the future? Explain.

2. Why do Jamie and Claudia want to go visit Mrs. Frankweiler secretly in the future?

3. What evidence is there that Saxonberg is the children's grandfather?

4. What do you think Mrs. Frankweiler feels about Mr. Saxonberg? Support your opinion with details from the story.

5. What is important to Mrs. Basil E. Frankweiler? What is important to Claudia? What is important to Jamie? What is important to Saxonberg?

Adopt a Grandparent. Mrs. Frankweiler was sad because she could never know what it was like to be a mother or a grandmother. Claudia and Jamie want to adopt Mrs. Frankweiler. What do you think she has to offer to a family? Describe what a grandmother does for a family.

Chapter 1

Write a Letter

In the beginning of the story we meet Mrs. Basil E. Frankweiler, who is writing a letter to her lawyer. She seems annoyed with him. As we read the story, we will see how this letter ties into the plot of the story. E. L. Konigsburg, created a very strong and memorable character and then had her write the letter. Now it's your turn. Imagine you are a different character. Think about whom this new you is. What is your personality, background, interests? Now think of a reason you may have to write a letter to someone else. Give that person a name, a title, a job. Maybe to complain about something, to thank someone, to find out information, to give them an order or some business. Just think of a good reason to write to the person. Now write the letter in 2 to 3 paragraphs as if you were the imaginary character. Use his or her voice; throw in detail about his or her life, likes, values etc. Make up a character's name for you to use in signing the letter.

Chapter 3

Newspaper Article

Write the newspaper article for the New York Times newspaper about Claudia and Jamie's disappearance. Newspaper articles should have a Headline that grabs people's attention, make yours sensational. The first paragraph should be short sentences and give only the most important information: Who? Did What? When? Where? Why? (if you know) How? (if you know) and for how long? In the second paragraph, include more background information: maybe what they took, a quick quote from parents, teachers, classmates, neighbors, bus driver etc. Include a picture that would go with your article.

Chapter 6

Do's and Don'ts According to Claudia

Claudia loves rules and order. She believes there is a right way and a wrong way to do things. Make a one-page poster of 10 rules by which Claudia tries to live. Go back through the book to find times where she has told Jamie what he should or shouldn't do. Make it look like the bulletin board or official rules signs that you see at parks, museums and swimming pools. You should come up with the title to write in big letters at the top of the rules poster. You may come up with some little graphics/images to make the poster more interesting. Imagine that people reading it may not speak English; have some symbols or pictures that would be easily understood.

Chapter 8

Theme

What do you think is the main idea for this story? The theme is the central idea or underlying message of the story. The theme is not simply said. To find the theme, you have to think about the plot, characters and setting. Some people have suggested that the theme in this book could be: growing up, fate, family, proving your worth, independence, and self-actualization. What do you think? Write a paragraph to say what you believe the theme is. Be sure to give facts and examples from the story.

Chapter 8

Dear Diary

Diaries or Journals are a great way to record what you did each day, and what your thoughts and feelings are at the time. They can also be used to record what money you spend each day. Pretend you are Jamie and Claudia and write an entry in a journal at the end of each day. Be sure to talk about the day from each child's perspective. What would Jamie spend time talking about? Jamie would feel very strongly about some events in the day. What would he hardly notice? Repeat the process with Claudia.

Chapter 9

Interview the Children

Mrs. Basil E. Frankweiler wanted to know what the children were doing for the last week. She wanted all the details. Imagine that you could sit in on the interview where she is asking all the questions. Think of 10 questions she would ask. Be careful to write the questions using her type of vocabulary and in her type of style, which shows her personality. Then, answer the questions using details from the story, and in the style of the person answering. Remember Claudia's personality and style of talking, or Jamie's grammar errors and favorite words and expressions.

NAME: ______________________________

Word Search Puzzle

Find the following words from the story. The words are written horizontally, vertically, diagonally, and some are written backwards.

auction	**furious**	**monotony**	**quarterly**	**treasurer**
automat	**genius**	**mysterious**	**shepherded**	**urged**
bequeathing	**humility**	**pagan**	**sissy**	**veto**
caper	**jostling**	**peck**	**stowaways**	**vow**
fidgeted	**mastaba**	**pinchpenny**	**tightwad**	**whiffs**

n	f	j	d	b	e	p	a	s	c	i	a	u	j	h	u	r	l	y	b	e	i	l	h
n	l	r	a	g	n	i	v	u	d	a	w	t	h	g	i	t	o	p	s	n	b	s	e
m	e	q	e	w	o	n	m	o	n	o	t	o	n	y	i	d	s	d	o	o	s	u	l
i	u	n	a	e	r	c	l	i	g	i	o	t	v	o	w	f	a	e	l	p	n	b	c
i	o	u	o	e	d	h	j	r	e	b	u	e	b	p	l	h	e	g	r	d	s	c	u
f	l	n	z	p	a	p	q	u	n	s	c	v	d	f	a	f	r	r	i	a	e	b	g
x	s	e	v	e	p	e	e	f	i	q	w	o	t	l	k	g	a	u	t	d	v	l	g
h	e	g	n	q	e	n	a	s	u	m	c	a	p	e	r	k	a	s	r	f	r	a	s
g	e	b	k	e	a	n	s	l	s	o	l	k	m	o	n	p	u	n	o	c	t	e	a
r	p	e	h	a	z	y	t	i	l	i	m	u	h	g	t	o	a	z	t	v	d	s	t
i	s	u	l	l	i	d	o	o	a	p	i	u	o	s	i	f	y	w	x	c	i	o	t
q	c	t	q	u	q	l	w	l	e	t	y	b	c	r	p	k	l	y	e	v	z	n	a
m	u	u	v	q	m	t	a	m	o	t	u	a	e	j	c	o	r	z	t	e	h	e	g
u	r	l	y	l	u	r	w	g	n	i	h	t	a	e	u	q	e	b	c	i	a	u	j
x	e	a	q	e	x	e	a	j	b	l	s	r	p	u	o	l	t	s	n	e	n	w	l
u	s	l	d	u	u	a	y	k	v	y	o	p	s	y	h	k	r	h	r	u	r	g	m
t	q	n	o	m	t	s	s	j	m	a	s	t	a	b	a	g	a	e	d	e	v	c	b
d	e	w	l	c	d	u	t	u	o	p	v	d	r	e	f	s	u	p	n	n	l	q	u
g	h	o	o	d	g	r	d	o	a	s	x	c	q	u	e	f	q	h	m	w	z	w	m
y	u	i	u	i	y	e	g	a	d	e	t	e	g	d	i	f	a	e	e	u	i	a	v
g	e	s	r	s	g	r	y	o	c	w	f	l	b	l	p	i	s	r	n	i	l	t	l
q	l	y	e	z	q	k	g	p	x	s	y	v	i	u	o	h	d	d	i	s	p	h	e
u	g	g	u	c	u	a	q	a	u	c	t	i	o	n	g	w	f	e	s	u	b	e	f
r	e	d	i	g	r	a	u	z	w	q	e	a	t	y	g	k	j	d	r	h	y	i	a

NAME: ____________________

Comprehension Quiz

29

Answer each question in a complete sentence.

1. Why did Claudia want to run away? 1

2. Why does she pick her brother Jamie to go with her? Give two reasons. 2

3. Summarize 3 steps Claudia took in planning her escape to the Art Museum in New York City. 3

4. Why was the mystery of the little Angel statue so important to Claudia? 2

5. List 2 ways Claudia and Jamie met their basic needs for Food and Shelter while hiding at the Museum. 2

6. Who is the narrator of the story? Why are they part of the story? 2

7. Contrast Claudia and Jamie's personality. Include at least 3 personality traits to compare. 3

SUBTOTAL: /15

After You Read

NAME: ______________________________

Comprehension Quiz

8. How was Saxonberg connected to the story and why did Mrs. Basil E. Frankweiler write to him?

____

______________________________ 2

9. How did the children take a bath and how did taking the bath solve their money problem?

____

______________________________ 2

10. How did the children solve the mystery of the stone Angel, and how did they tell the people at the museum?

______________________________ 3

____

11. What was the peak or climax of the plot?

______________________________ 1

____

12. How was Mrs. Basil E. Frankweiler similar to Jamie?

____

______________________________ 2

13. How was Mrs. Basil E. Frankweiler similar to Claudia?

______________________________ 2

____

14. What does Mrs. Frankweiler give to Claudia, and why does it allow her to go home feeling important?

____

______________________________ 2

____

SUBTOTAL: /14

1.
Answers will vary.

2.
Answers will vary.

Vocabulary

1. D
2. J
3. A
4. C
5. I
6. G
7. B
8. H
9. E
10. F

1.

a) ✓ C

b) ✓ D

c) ✓ C

d) ✓ A

e) ✓ D

1.
Mrs. Basil E. Frankweiler is telling the story. She explains in the letter that she is writing to her lawyer to change her will.

2.
Answers will vary.

3.
Answers will vary, but may include: Claudia isn't really sure, but she feels that she has to do more because she is the oldest and a girl AND she is tired of the boring life she is living.

4.
Answers will vary.

5.
Answers will vary, but may include: He had money, he had a radio, "he was good for a laugh".

6.
Answers will vary, but may include: "You just may get your wish." Claudia says to Kevin, when he says he wishes he was always Steve's responsibility.

1.
Answers will vary, but may include: She likes to plan and enjoys doing something different.

2.
Answers will vary.

Vocabulary

1. ragged
2. percolator
3. racket
4. thoroughness
5. Expenditures
6. terminal
7. Sissy
8. traveler's checks

1.

a) 4
b) 6
c) 5
d) 7
e) 2
f) 3
g) 1

2.

a) F
b) F
c) T
d) F
e) T
f) F
g) T
h) F

1.
Answers will vary, but may include: Mrs. Frankweiler also appreciates attention to detail.

2.
Answers will vary, but may include: He says he likes complications, and he is picturing what a secret agent would do. He wants this adventure.

3.
Claudia cares about her parents and doesn't want them to worry. She mails the box tops away for money, because she is planning on coming home.

4.
Jamie thought they were going to hide out in the woods. That seemed like a great adventure to him, like camping.

5.
This hints again that Mrs. Frankweiler and Claudia share similarities. Both of them felt small and scared when they came out of the train terminal into the big bustling city.

6.
She realizes that the city is big.

EZ✓

© CLASSROOM COMPLETE PRESS

EZ✓

1.
Answers will vary.

2.
Answers will vary.

Vocabulary

1. mimicked

2. extravagant

3. accumulation

4. cheapskate

5. carbon dioxide

6. veto

7. inconspicuous

8. tyrannical.

(17)

1.

a) ✓ A

b) ✓ B

c) ✓ D

d) ✓ A

e) ✓ B

f) ✓ B

(18)

1.
Gentle old ladies, tourists, and art students.

2.
She is trying to make Saxonberg realize that he too should go to the Art museum with her.

3.
Saxonberg is the person the narrator is writing to. We know that he is her lawyer, he works with tax law, and apparently is only interested in work and his grandchildren.

4.
They are going to hide in the bathrooms and then sneak back to the French bed with a canopy, and sleep there. They have a good plan for getting in and finding a place to sleep, and a way to hide from the security.

5.
They were tired because running away was stressful and exciting. They walked 40 blocks to the museum.

6.
They were quiet, in the dark, behind the canopy on the bed, and he was not expecting anyone to be sleeping in the museum.

(19)

Vocabulary

Across

1. enormous
3. dreaded
6. sarcophagus
10. emerge
12. hodge
13. whiff
14. urn
15. stash
18. imposter
19. vat

Down

2. mediocre
4. drape
5. essence
7. glimpse
8. smoldering
9. petticoat
11. glorification
15. smug
16. automat
17. barrier

(20)

1.

a) scatter, officials

b) sarcophagus, tapestry, urn, drape

c) slight, visitor, janitor, wringing

d) delighted, danger,

e) important, mystery

2.

a) 1

b) 5

c) 2

d) 3

e) 6

f) 4

(21)

1.
"Like empty tubes of toothpaste."

2.
Answers will vary, but may include: They run to the museum; they find a place to hide their things; Jamie almost gets caught; they were hungry.

3.
He thought his sister would get sick of the Italian Renaissance because it was so big.

4.
Saxonberg works with taxes, he looks at photo albums of his grandchildren, he isn't a romantic like Mrs. Frankweiler and like Claudia.

5.
She is still making rules for lessons, organizing tooth brushing etc. She is still looking after Jamie.

6.
Answers will vary, but may include: Mrs. Frankweiler understands Claudia and shares a romantic nature with her. They are both captivated by the artistic genius of Michelangelo.

(22)

© CLASSROOM COMPLETE PRESS

1.
Answers will vary.

2.
Answers will vary.

Vocabulary

1. C

2. E

3. F

4. H

5. D

6. G

7. B

8. A

(23)

1.

a) ✓ A

b) ✓ D

c) ✓ C

d) ✓ B

e) ✓ A

f) ✓ C

(24)

1.
Answers will vary, but may include: He was a good companion; he didn't get mad when she was grouchy; he was observant and upbeat during the research; he played with her in the park and he went along with her plans.

2.
Answers will vary, but may include: It shows how Jamie likes to tease her and he is a bit reckless or adventurous; there are real dangers out there, and there are dangers in running away from home.

3.
Claudia is a romantic: she is in love with the beauty and mystery of the statue.

4.
At first, Jamie thought they must have no conscience, but after Claudia explained that it was because they were so well adjusted, he seemed satisfied with her explanation.

5.
Answers will vary, but may include: She is trying to feel different. Her satisfaction with how well she answered the question makes her feel grown up.

(25)

1.
Answers will vary, but may include: Mrs. Frankweiler owned the angel.

2.
Answers will vary, but may include: They might spend more money.

Vocabulary

1. stealthily

2. quarters

3. stonemason

4. shepherded

5. telegrams

6. descending

7. furious

8. pinchpenny

(26)

1.

a) F

b) T

c) F

d) T

e) T

f) T

g) F

h) T

2.

a) statue

b) circles

c) stonemason

d) letter

(27)

1.
Jamie makes fun of Claudia for wanting to hug the statue. He doesn't understand his sister's love of the statue.

2.
Answers will vary.

3.
Claudia is more focused on how she can prove that Michelangelo carved the statue and thereby become a famous hero, rather than worrying about getting caught.

4.
Answers will vary.

5.
Answers will vary, but may include: Claudia started the story treating Jamie like a 'younger brother'; now she talks to him more like an equal partner in the adventure. They joke around more, they accept each other's personality quirks, and they support each other.

EZ✓

(28)

© CLASSROOM COMPLETE PRESS

EZ✓

29

1.
Answers will vary.

Vocabulary

1. H
2. C
3. F
4. B
5. I
6. J
7. A
8. G
9. E
10. D

30

1.
a) 6
b) 7
c) 5
d) 2
e) 1
f) 4
g) 3

2.
a) mailbox, breakfast
b) student, mastaba
c) liked, climate/time
d) mastaba, teacher/classmates
e) put, talked
f) perfect, letter
g) collapsed, yikes

31

1.
Claudia really wanted to become known for solving the mystery. She felt it would make her important.

2.
Claudia sees the advantage of Jamie taking the letter in himself and saying he is from the school he is from. They don't have to trust that a student would take the letter in, and they don't have to trust that the student would not notice what they looked like.

3.
He didn't want to get caught.

4.
Answers will vary.

5.
Answers will vary.

32

1.
Answers will vary.

2.
Answers will vary.

Vocabulary

1. counterfeit
2. topaz
3. keen
4. sarcastic
5. consensus
6. appreciate
7. righteously
8. fidgeted
9. disclosing

33

1.
a) F
b) T
c) F
d) T
e) F
f) F
g) T
h) F
i) F
j) T

2.
Answers will vary, but may include:
DID: his stonemason's mark on the bottom of the statue; Michelangelo's letter; it matches his style and skills.
DID NOT: he didn't carve every stone block that he bought; there could be people who copied him; it could have been carved by one of his students.

34

1.
Answers will vary, but may include: The guards and the cafeteria staff because it's not usual that kids would come back so often.

2.
Answers will vary, but may include: She could be herself somewhere different, or she could wear different clothing but live at home.

3.
Answers will vary, but may include: The letter was so polite, it was hard for her to be angry. If she was angry, she wouldn't feel so disappointed because the anger would distract her.

4.
Jamie was looking for an adventure. Now that it is getting a bit boring and uncomfortable he can go home.

5.
Claudia wanted to be different, she thought that just a change of places would make her different, but she realized that she is still the same no matter where she goes.

6.
Claudia has become more humble and acts on a hunch. Jamie understands how important this is for Claudia and supports her.

© CLASSROOM COMPLETE PRESS

1.

Mrs. Frankweiler is rich; she loves the Art Museum; she used to own the Angel sculpture; she has a tax lawyer named Saxonberg; she is changing her will.

2.

Answers will vary.

Vocabulary

1. D

2. A

3. E

4. C

5. F

6. G

7. H

8. I

9. J

10. B

35

1.

a) B

b) A

c) A

d) C

e) A

36

1.

Her house is cluttered with antiques and valuable art. Her office is like a laboratory: clean, bright, and with 17 filing cabinets lining one wall. Answers will vary.

2.

She was completing some research about the children and she wanted to set the tone of their meeting.

3.

She is old, her nose is longish, her hair is cut by her butler, she is wearing an expensive pearl necklace and lab coat. Her way of speaking is very direct and gruff. She says she doesn't like wasting time.

4.

She likes how Claudia is smart and will hold onto information to exchange for knowledge from Mrs. Frankweiler. She also liked that Claudia was determined.

5.

The children were given 1 hour to find the file with the proof of the Angel. They have to figure out Mrs. Frankweiler's filing system, in order to find the file.

6.

Answers will vary.

37

1.

Answers will vary.

2.

Answers will vary.

Vocabulary

1. intercom

2. accurate

3. preoccupied

4. maimed

5. bequeathing

6. matron

7. chariot

8. tight

9. auction

38

1.

a) tape recorder

b) parents

c) tour

d) chauffeur/driver

e) angel

f) excitement, secret, fun

g) Mrs. Frankweiler

h) adopt

2.

1. Mrs. Frankweiler

2. Sheldon the Chauffeur

3. Jamie

4. Jamie

5. Claudia

6. Claudia

7. Kevin

8. Commissioner of Parks in New York City.

39

1.

Answers will vary.

2.

Jamie would like the adventure of sneaking away to Mrs. Frankweiler's and Claudia would like to plan the trip and have another secret.

3.

From the first letter, all the way through, Mrs. Frankweiler mentions his concern for his grandchildren. Then he is the one who calls the parents. Mrs. Frankweiler says that they are his grandchildren, and then the chauffeur sees Saxonberg in the children's house.

4.

Answers will vary, but may include: She wants him to enjoy the art museum with her; she wants him to relax; she says that she will be a grandmother, and he's the grandfather, so that is hinting that she likes him.

5.

Mrs. Frankweiler likes to investigate mysteries and to gather experiences. Claudia likes comfort and having knowledge. Jamie likes to have fun, adventure, and 'complications'. Saxonberg loves his grandchildren and tax law.

EZ

40

© CLASSROOM COMPLETE PRESS

Word Search Puzzle

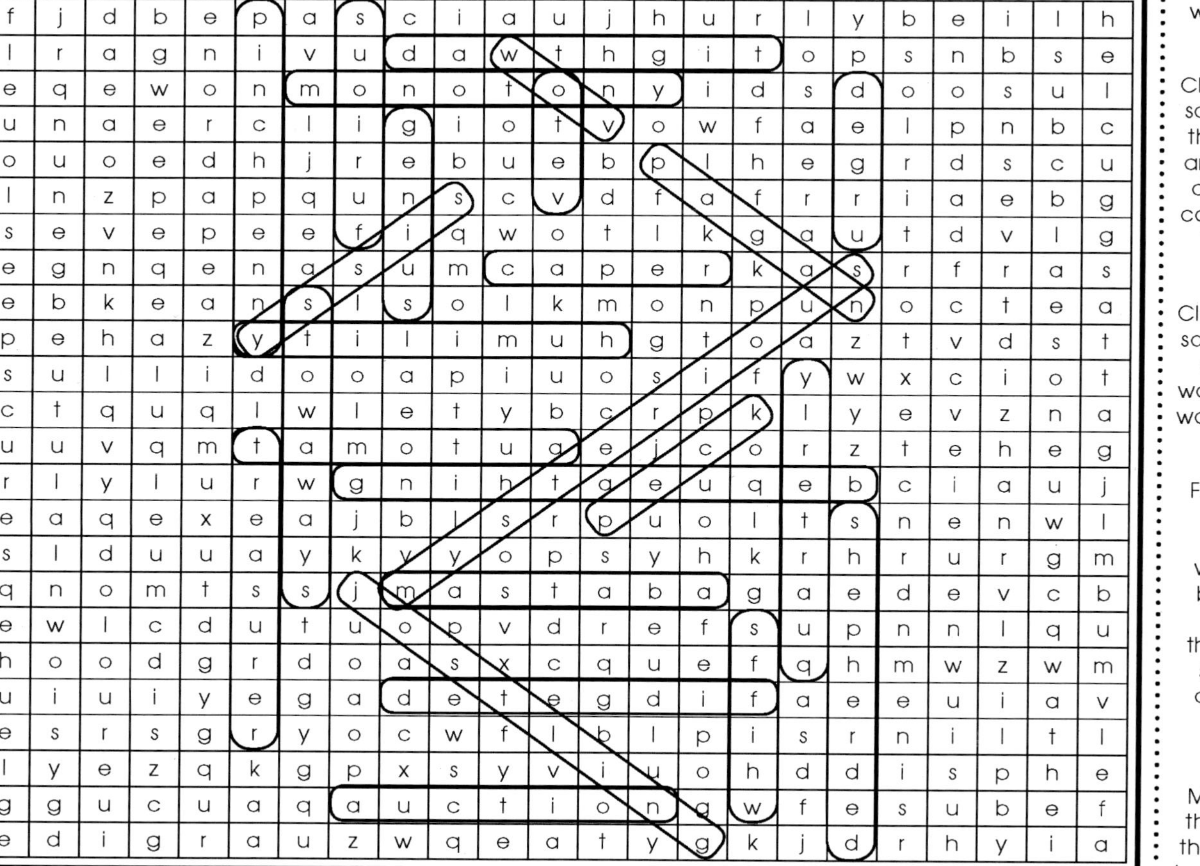

1.
Claudia wanted out of the monotony.

2.
She chose Jamie because he had money and a radio, and she felt he could keep a secret and was up for an adventure.

3.
Claudia cut out treats and saved money, she studied the map for the museum, and she planned the best day to go because they could pack their clothes in their instrument cases.

4.
Claudia thought that if she solved the mystery of who carved the statue, she would be famous and that would make her important.

5.
For food, they ate at the museum with classes and their other meals were from the automat because it was cheap. For shelter, they hid in the bathrooms and then selected a bed with a canopy curtain to hide behind.

6.
Mrs. Basil E. Frankweiler is the narrator, she is telling the story in a 'letter to her lawyer' to explain how she met the children.

7.
Claudia: fussy, particular, cautious. Jamie: carefree, risk taker/adventurous, pinchpenny, adaptable, funny.

8.
Saxonberg is Mrs. Frankweiler's lawyer, but also the grandfather to Claudia and Jamie. She wrote to him to tell him where his grandchildren were.

9.
They take a bath in the fountain and find coins that people have left,

10.
They found a record of the carved symbol Michelangelo marked on his stone. They rented a post office box and left a letter at the Museum office asking them to respond to the post office box so they can stay anonymous.

11.
When the children decided to go ask Mrs. Basil E. Frankweiler about the stone Angel.

12.
They played cards (and cheated) and was 'thrifty'.

13.
They liked elegance and to plan with detail.

14.
Mrs. Frankweiler gives the secret of the stone Angel to Claudia, but only if she keeps the secret until after Mrs. Frankweiler dies.

© CLASSROOM COMPLETE PRESS

Venn Diagram

Compare two characters from the story. Write the character names in the circles. Write down any differences the characters have in the outside circles. Write down any similarities the characters have in the space where the circles overlap. Suggested characters to compare: Claudia, Mrs. Basil E. Frankweiler, Jamie, Saxonberry.

© CLASSROOM COMPLETE PRESS

Map Out the Children's Journey

Map the children's journey on the plot pyramid. Start with the introduction in the children's home. Then, describe the rising action and then the climax. Follow with the falling action and then the conclusion. Finish up by describing how the author ties up any loose ends in the story in the denouement.

Climax

Rising Action

Falling Action

Introduction

Conclusion

Denouement

Literary Elements

Outline the literary elements used in this story. Describe the tone, mood, purpose, audience, writing style, and theme. In each file folder, record details and quotes from the story that support each literary device.

Tone

Mood

Purpose

Audience

Writing Style

Theme

- **RSL.5.1** Quote accurately from a text when explaining what the text says explicitly and when drawing inferences from the text.
- **RSL.5.2** Determine a theme of a story, drama, or poem from details in the text, including how characters in a story or drama respond to challenges or how the speaker in a poem reflects upon a topic; summarize the text.
- **RSL.5.3** Compare and contrast two or more characters, settings, or events in a story or drama, drawing on specific details in the text.
- **RSL.5.4** Determine the meaning of words and phrases as they are used in a text, including figurative language such as metaphors and similes.
- **RSL.5.5** Explain how a series of chapters, scenes, or stanzas fits together to provide the overall structure of a particular story, drama, or poem.
- **RSL.5.6** Describe how a narrator's or speaker's point of view influences how events are described.
- **RSL.5.9** Compare and contrast stories in the same genre on their approaches to similar themes and topics.
- **RSL.5.10** By the end of the year read and comprehend literature, including stories, dramas, and poetry, at the high end of the grades 4–5 text complexity band independently and proficiently.
- **RSL.6.1** Cite textual evidence to support analysis of what the text says explicitly as well as inferences drawn from the text.
- **RSL.6.2** Determine a theme or central idea of a text and how it is conveyed through particular details; provide a summary of the text distinct from personal opinions or judgments.
- **RSL.6.3** Describe how a particular story's or drama's plot unfolds in a series of episodes as well as how the characters respond or change as the plot moves toward a resolution.
- **RSL.6.4** Determine the meaning of words and phrases as they are used in a text, including figurative and connotative meanings; analyze the impact of a specific word choice on meaning and tone.
- **RSL.6.5** Analyze how a particular sentence, chapter, scene, or stanza fits into the overall structure of a text and contributes to the development of the theme, setting, or plot.
- **RSL.6.6** Explain how an author develops the point of view of the narrator or speaker in a text.
- **RSL.6.10** By the end of the year read and comprehend literature, including stories, dramas, and poems, in the grades 6–8 text complexity band proficiently, with scaffolding as needed at the high end of the range.
- **RSFS.5.3** Know and apply grade-level phonics and word analysis skills in decoding words. **A)** Use combined knowledge of all letter-sound correspondences, syllabication patterns, and morphology to read accurately unfamiliar multisyllabic words in context and out of context.
- **RSFS.5.4** Read with sufficient accuracy and fluency to support comprehension. **A)** Read grade-level text with purpose and understanding. **B)** Read grade-level prose and poetry orally with accuracy, appropriate rate, and expression on successive readings. **C)** Use context to confirm or self-correct word recognition and understanding, rereading as necessary.
- **WS.5.1** Write opinion pieces on topics or texts, supporting a point of view with reasons and information. **A)** Introduce a topic or text clearly, state an opinion, and create an organizational structure in which ideas are logically grouped to support the writer's purpose. **B)** Provide logically ordered reasons that are supported by facts and details. **C)** Link opinion and reasons using words, phrases, and clauses. **D)** Provide a concluding statement or section related to the opinion presented.
- **WS.5.2** Write informative/explanatory texts to examine a topic and convey ideas and information clearly. **A)** Introduce a topic clearly, provide a general observation and focus, and group related information logically; include formatting, illustrations, and multimedia when useful to aiding comprehension. **B)** Develop the topic with facts, definitions, concrete details, quotations, or other information and examples related to the topic. **C)** Link ideas within and across categories of information using words, phrases, and clauses. **D)** Use precise language and domain-specific vocabulary to inform about or explain the topic. **E)** Provide a concluding statement or section related to the information or explanation presented.
- **WS.5.3** Write narratives to develop real or imagined experiences or events using effective technique, descriptive details, and clear event sequences. Orient the reader by establishing a situation and introducing a narrator and/or characters; organize an event sequence that unfolds naturally. **B)** Use narrative techniques, such as dialogue, description, and pacing, to develop experiences and events or show the responses of characters to situations. **C)** Use a variety of transitional words, phrases, and clauses to manage the sequence of events. **D)** Use concrete words and phrases and sensory details to convey experiences and events precisely. **E)** Provide a conclusion that follows from the narrated experiences or events.
- **WS.5.4** Produce clear and coherent writing in which the development and organization are appropriate to task, purpose, and audience.
- **WS.5.7** Conduct short research projects that use several sources to build knowledge through investigation of different aspects of a topic.
- **WS.5.8** Recall relevant information from experiences or gather relevant information from print and digital sources; summarize or paraphrase information in notes and finished work, and provide a list of sources.
- **WS.5.9** Recall relevant information from experiences or gather relevant information from print and digital sources; summarize or paraphrase information in notes and finished work, and provide a list of sources.
- **WS.6.1** Write arguments to support claims with clear reasons and relevant evidence. **A)** Introduce claim(s) and organize the reasons and evidence clearly. **B)** Support claim(s) with clear reasons and relevant evidence, using credible sources and demonstrating an understanding of the topic or text. **C)** Use words, phrases, and clauses to clarify the relationships among claim(s) and reasons. **D)** Establish and maintain a formal style. **E)** Provide a concluding statement or section that follows from the argument presented.
- **WS.6.2** Write informative/explanatory texts to examine a topic and convey ideas, concepts, and information through the selection, organization, and analysis of relevant content. **A)** Introduce a topic; organize ideas, concepts, and information, using strategies such as definition, classification, comparison/contrast, and cause/effect; include formatting, graphics, and multimedia when useful to aiding comprehension. **B)** Develop the topic with relevant facts, definitions, concrete details, quotations, or other information and examples. **C)** Use appropriate transitions to clarify the relationships among ideas and concepts. **D)** Use precise language and domain-specific vocabulary to inform about or explain the topic. **E)** Establish and maintain a formal style. **F)** Provide a concluding statement or section that follows from the information or explanation presented.
- **WS.6.3** Write narratives to develop real or imagined experiences or events using effective technique, relevant descriptive details, and well-structured event sequences. **A)** Engage and orient the reader by establishing a context and introducing a narrator and/or characters; organize an event sequence that unfolds naturally and logically. **B)** Use narrative techniques, such as dialogue, pacing, and description, to develop experiences, events, and/or characters. **C)** Use a variety of transition words, phrases, and clauses to convey sequence and signal shifts from one time frame or setting to another. **D)** Use precise words and phrases, relevant descriptive details, and sensory language to convey experiences and events. **E)** Provide a conclusion that follows from the narrated experiences or events.
- **WS.6.4** Produce clear and coherent writing in which the development, organization, and style are appropriate to task, purpose, and audience.
- **WS.6.7** Conduct short research projects to answer a question, drawing on several sources and refocusing the inquiry when appropriate.
- **WS.6.8** Gather relevant information from multiple print and digital sources; assess the credibility of each source; and quote or paraphrase the data and conclusions of others while avoiding plagiarism and providing basic bibliographic information for sources.
- **WS.6.9** Draw evidence from literary or informational texts to support analysis, reflection, and research. **A)** Apply *grade 6 Reading standards* to literature. **B)** Apply *grade 6 Reading standards* to literary nonfiction.